Wid Kattan is a poet, writer and mother. She works as a psychiatrist, therapist and life coach, and specializes in women's mental health and wellness. She trained in Canada and works in Saudi Arabia. Her empathic way of helping others through her work is firmly rooted in her personal as well as her professional experience.

So Many Hats (or Veils)

Wid Kattan

AUSTIN MACAULEY PUBLISHERS™

LONDON • CAMBRIDGE • NEW YORK • SHARJAH

ISBN – 9789948354444 – (Paperback)
ISBN – 9789948354437 – (E-Book)

Application Number: MC-10-01-6633199
Age Classification: 17+

The age group that matches the content of the books has been classified according to the age classification system issued by the National Media Council.

First Published (2020)
AUSTIN MACAULEY PUBLISHERS FZE
Sharjah Publishing City
P.O Box (519201)
Sharjah, UAE
www.austinmacauley.ae
+971 655 95 202

This book is dedicated to:
Me

I know. The audacity.
You should try it though.

I would like to thank everyone who has helped this book come to light, from the stranger who encouraged me to write, to the friend who encouraged me to share. Thank you for being a part of my life experience, for inspiring my writing, for accompanying me on my journey, for cheering me on, for giving me feedback and, most of all, for believing in me and in this book.

I thank God first. For everything. I thank my mother for teaching me to love books, and my father—may his soul rest in peace—for seeing the writer in me. I thank the professionals who helped polish this book: Eschler Editing for their editorial services, Ida Fia Sveningsson for the book cover design, Shaker Kashgari for my personal logo, Vivian Doan for the author's photo, Hassan Tayeb for his help with design and marketing, and Austin Macauley for their publishing services. You helped make this book a work of art. Thanks also goes to the UAE National Media Council and Sharjah Publishing City in general, and to Ibrahim Khadim in particular for genuinely helping authors' voices reach far and wide.

Thank you, dear sisters: Thuraya, Nad, Dur, Walaa and Leen, for being my soft place to fall. Thank you, dear brothers Abdullah and Mohammed, for being my solid place to lean. Thank you, Dur, for being my first reader and my role model when it comes to street smarts and coolness. Thank you, Thuraya, for illustrating "Evergreen". Other contributors to the illustrations are my children: Abdulrahman, thank you for drawing "this moon", and, Omar, thank you for drawing "these stars". You are my stars. Mariam, my daughter, deserves thanks for inspiring many poems in the "Individual" and "Woman" chapters. Thank you for being such a superstar and for reminding me how to be myself.

I have another family to thank, the one that provided the space and support for me to grow and for this work to be born: In-laws—thank you.

Nouf, Reem, Rawan and Sara: you gave me invaluable friendly and professional input and encouragement.

Barbara, Alanna, Arlene, Eric (and the boys): you are my home away from home.

Maria, Areej, Sarah, Julie, Annie, Najd and Broog: you are marble-jar friends.

Rozana and my daring friends: you got me in the Arena. Please stay in the front seats that will always be reserved for you.

To all my friends who read, follow, give feedback, inspire, listen and who are just…there. I am grateful to you.

Last but not least: Fadi.

Thank you for being my tech support

and my life support.

CONTENTS

INTRODUCTION

I am human, and nothing of that which is
human is alien to me.

Terence in *Heauton Timorumenos*

I'd like to introduce myself to you before you read my poems. I'm a woman, psychiatrist, life coach, and writer. I'm a Muslim, a mother, and many other things. I sometimes see myself as a juggler trying to keep all the balls in the air (I've learned to stop and set some down, or else they start dropping like the rain). Or as a chameleon shifting colours, transforming as I cross the thresholds of my roles.

I've always loved hats, so the metaphor of hats representing the various roles we play in life appeals to me. Wearing hats is less hectic than juggling and more deliberate than a chameleon's changing colours. You can see a person's eyes under their hat, and so they can remain themselves, authentic and real. The veil is just one of my hats, though the world today seems determined to give it so much weight that on some days, it actually feels quite heavy.

The poems in this book are divided into seven sections and are based on the theme of the seven hats I wear: Human, Individual, Writer, Woman, Mother, Romantic, and Muslim.

You may find that the voice and illustrations differ from one chapter, or page, to another. Some poems seemed to need titles; others seemed to outright refuse them. The truth is, I organically wrote and drew what came to my mind and have decided not to overfilter or overthink the consistency of the content because human nature is complex and messy and contradictory. I *do* feel differently when wearing different hats, so it seems natural to just let myself *sound* different—sound how I feel. The other reason the book may feel wavy is that writing it has been an exercise in defying my perfectionism. I drew with my daughter on my lap and typed with one hand if the other was busy, and when a sketch didn't fit onto a page, I left it unfinished because that is life; and if you don't keep going, you'll never finish anything. Presenting you with this book, with all its unpolished rawness, isn't meant to be lazy or careless. I hope you'll see it as authentic and brave.

Some chapters are shorter, like "Woman" and "Individual". For reasons I'm still figuring out, I find it hard to articulate what it means to be a woman, and I'm still rediscovering who I am as an individual. Some chapters are long, like the "Human" chapter. I find writing under this hat the easiest, but I guess that's natural. After all, it's the most basic aspect of who we are.

There is deliberately no psychiatrist, therapist, or life-coach hat in this book. I try to wear my "human" hat to the office. When I write a poem about depression, for example, I don't feel I'm describing a disorder; I feel like I'm describing a very common human experience.

Still, I believe that working in mental health helps me be a better writer and human being. It has given me the opportunity to travel and to live and work in my home country of Saudi Arabia and in Canada, where I studied and trained. Being exposed to different cultures at the intimate level one can only reach through therapy has been such a gift, such a teacher of how to develop a flexible perspective and become a more global citizen.

In my office, people come wearing different "hats". I have seen Orthodox Jewish women in their wigs; Muslim women in their hijabs; intimidating businessmen in their well-cut suits; and tough, gruff Arab men in their "shemaghs" (headdress). They all come into my office and may eventually trust me enough to let their guards down, and then may wearily take off their hats and rest them on my desk. Sometimes they rest their bald heads, too. When we look into each other's eyes, all our fancy hats don't matter. We're all so tired. We recognize each other, and we sometimes cry together, for our common suffering and for all of humanity.

I believe we don't need to be the same in every way in order to connect. We only need to recognize each other at one level to care about each other. We need to have only one hat, one experience in common, for us to realise we are essentially the same. If we can see each other as parents, as women, as *human,* that's enough. If we share a loss, a fear, a hope, that's enough. This is a valuable truth I've learned in therapy and in life, and I want to share it with you through writing and poetry.

To Sum Up This Book and Who I Am

There has never before
lived anyone
like me—or you
we are so different
yet so the same

That's all you need to know
about me, because
this book is not really
about you knowing me
it's about you
feeling *known*
and a little less
alone

I hope you find some part of
yourself here
on these pages
with me.
I'm me
and I'm you.

Windows

Underneath
all my hats
my eyes—
they stay the
same:

Windows
into my soul.
that's who
"I"
am

I am not
any of my hats
or roles

Just another
kindred
soul.

Chapter 1
Human

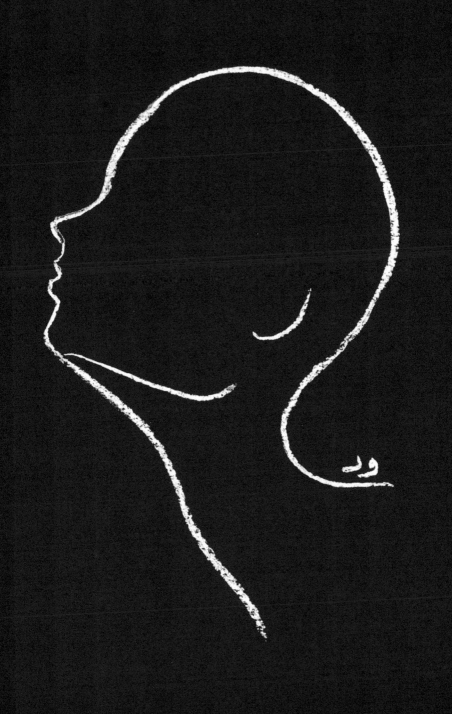

We are all born—and most of us will be buried—without hats on our heads. During the course of our lives, we experience many similar stories related to friendship, betrayal, loss, grief, moving, the seasons, nature, and change. We experience...common human experiences.

That's what this chapter is about. As with the other chapters, some poems come from my own life (I talk a lot about moving and goodbyes), while others are inspired by the collective people I help, listen to, or observe from a distance. When I accompany someone on their journey, I walk in their shoes, hold their hand, and try to be a witness to their life. I have the privilege of glimpsing their heartache and heartbreak, even if I do not truly know the depth of their sorrow. I may mean it differently than he did, but Mark Twain said it well: 'I've lived through some terrible things in my life, some of which actually happened.'

Since many of the themes explored in this chapter are themes I may explore with someone in therapy, I toyed—for about a minute—with the idea of giving it the name or hat of "Psychiatrist". I decided against it for two reasons: a selfless and a selfish one.

Selfless first: I believe it is most helpful to people, whether in therapy or in poetry, when the person before them is human and humble. I'm okay with some self-disclosure and some sharing and some tears. Shared for the right reasons, it can make the most valuable and healing of gifts.[1]

My selfish reason? I don't want to be a professional psychiatrist here. This is my book, my baby. I want to be myself. In fact, I will make this chapter a stepping-stone to being more authentic, always, in real life, including when I am at the office.

Some context: Ever since I returned to Saudi a year ago, I have been introduced as "The-doctor-psychiatrist-life-coach-specializing-in-women's-wellness-who-trained-in Canadaaaaaaa!"

---

[1] Irvin Yalom's books on therapy, including *The Gift of Therapy* (New York: Harper, 2002), have taught me a lot about existential therapy with a humanistic approach.

People have responded to this introduction by jokingly asking me to "analyse" them or by sincerely asking for my help. I became constantly on duty, under scrutiny, and too-often dragged into consultations at baby showers and social dinners. It became difficult to make new friends and to open up to some of my old ones. Many people expected me to be okay, to have it all together *all* the time, and to be constantly upbeat and positive and cheerful, or else I was teased with: 'Aren't you supposed to be the psychiatrist?'

How often have I heard this Arabic saying, one I have come to loathe: 'The carpenter's door is broken.'

Wow. It was tough to be under that sort of pressure when *I had just moved my entire life*. I left behind so much, and my hands were still empty in this new place. Do people honestly expect mental health professionals (and all doctors, for that matter) to achieve perfection and to maintain it in all areas of life before offering their services?

Disclaimer: I by no means claim perfection. In fact, I make mistakes every day. I feel, deeply, all sorts of messy and ugly feelings. I believe that helps me help others deal with their own ugly, messy feelings. I proudly own my battle scars. They make me a better psychiatrist and a better person. They make me human.

This chapter is my attempt at blurring the lines
between helper and client
between doctor and patient
between "normal" and "abnormal".

The carpenter's door
is not broken.
It's just

open.

Trauma

If I speak of it, will it swell?
if I bring it forth, will it dwell?
to examine it, reimagine it
is torture, a kind of hell
but to hold it in
makes the void within
an echoing, bottomless well

So...

should I carry it
and just bury it?
should I keep it in...
or tell?

The Dream

To be heard
to be seen
that's the beginning
of the dream

To be known
then accepted
after you've been
truly seen

To give your all
let yourself fall
bare your chest out
to the world

To sing your song
pour out your soul
let your rainbow wings
unfurl

To gift your heart
on the palm
of your hand
for those who may
—or may not—
understand

They may love you
they may hate you
they may rip you up
at the seams

But you might
just reach
someone out there
who shares
your unspoken
dream

To be heard
to be seen
is after all
what we all
hopefully
secretly

dream.

Moving

I peel it off the walls
ever so gently
the scotch-taped
colourful
artwork of their childhood

But no matter how careful I am
a layer peels off
a layer of paint
of pain

Sometimes the glue (or our attachment)
is so strong
that we can't say goodbye
without snatching a piece of home with us
or leaving a piece of us
behind
just to say:
we were here.

The Walls

As the walls grow bare
my heart grows heavy.

Rain

When it rains
on ending days
you know the ones
days like today

It feels like...
it's not just me
who wants
to stay

—a little longer

But the sky
and clouds
and that slanting ray

Are sad too
to see me
go away.

I am simply a guide
who sometimes
still gets lost.

Fall

I feel my heart fall
as the leaves fall
in my last fall
in Montreal

I feel my heart break
it's so high stakes
wish time would slow
to a crawl

It's my last shot
in the pool game
it's the black one
eight ball

But I'm going home
to remake a home
I won't be alone
after all

Still, it's so unknown
though it's called my own
have faith, close your eyes
freefa
    a
        a
          a
            a
              a
                a

Snow

Today, I witnessed
my last first snow
my first now seems
so long ago

I was not prepared then—
no hat, no gloves
head tipped back
heart warm with love

I'm not prepared now
to say goodbye
so this time
as it snows...

I cry.

November

Of all the months and days...
I've always loved November
writers' pencils softer now
not as sharp as in September

Fall colours
crisp air
I witness life
but am no member

Stolen moments
ephemeral
never lasting
dying ember

Nostalgia
possibility
pregnant pauses
to remember

But I mostly love...
the hope held in...
these last days...
before

December.

Drifting

I am a small boat
half ready to set sail
heavy
because I travel
so light

I'm tethered still to the shore
by many strings attached
not allowed to go
just yet

I wish I could
set sail today
Just go

Instead of this aimless drifting
to and fro
to and fro
to and fro

I'd rather seek out
that beautiful
terrifying
endless horizon
and vast open sea of unknown

I'd rather face that
than face...
the faces
on the shore
waving
waiting
waiting for that final goodbye.

Home

Where is home?
is home where you were born?
is it where you wish to die?
is it where you wish to live in between?
is it where you find yourself?
is it the one you love?
is home something you carry with you in your soul?
is it all of these things?
what if these things are scattered all over the earth...
and buried under it?

Someone once said to me:
once you've crossed the ocean
you feel you're always on the wrong side...

I think she was right.

Sentimental

I'm such
a sentimental thing
a girl who
cannot help but bring

Across the world
a little toy
meant for a little
girl or boy

A puppet
that her father bought
now tangled up
and full of knots

See, every single
business trip
he'd sneak into her room
and slip

A gift
from Hamley's
at her feet
and tuck her in
her Carebear sheets

That's how this puppet
came to be
a symbol
of his love for me

And now I pack
her tangled limbs
to go back home
but not to him.

Space

I need a place to unpack my bags
the bags under my eyes
a place to rest my head
my own pillow on which to cry

I want a home of my own
to roam as I please within
when the kids are at school
where I can scream and can sing

At the top of my lungs
where I can stretch out my arms
where I can let out the storms
so I can find my own calm

I need space   space   space
and more space for me to grow
I need room to run and race
I need time to get to know

Who I am, who I'll be
who I'm becoming in this place
to decide amongst new people
if their dreams are worth the chase

Or if my own dreams
you know; those old ones
the ones that are
now hard to trace

Are the real ones
but where are they?
packed away still...
stowed away still...
in my dusty old
suitcase...

Homesick

Wherever I go
I am homesick

it may simply be that
I haven't found my home
out there

but I fear that
I am simply lost
in here.

Akathisia

When I'm with people
I need to be alone
when alone
I seek people out
that is
the restlessness
the "akathisia"[2]
of grief.

---

[2] Akathisia is a movement disorder characterized by a feeling of inner restlessness and an inability to stay still. (See "Akathinsia." Wikipedia. Accessed April 2, 2019. https://en.wikipedia.org/wiki/Akathisia.)

Depression

No, no, don't open your eyes
not another one
not another day
torturous consciousness
please stay away

Don't wake up
fall back into a— please—dreamless sleep
or one with nightmares
as long as it's deep

Oblivion is better
'cause I'm afraid to discover
if I wake...
I'll put myself
to sleep
forever.

A Depression in My Mattress

There is a depression
in my mattress
that is
me

I am sinking in deep
unable to get up
or move

Gravity feels so powerful
it even explains
the state of my eyelids
horizontally shut

Sealed and gritty
no longer shedding tears
tears are alive
there is no life here

I pull the duvet
above my head
and its heaviness
echoes my own
laden
paralysis

I want to hide in the dark
in the night
where I am not missed
or expected
or awaited
or wanted

When they are all asleep at night
I breathe a little
I'm at last
not hurting anyone
with my presence
or my absence

The only time I am free
is when they all sleep
and so does their need for me

But morning comes

Go away day
leave me alone
don't look at me
or ask anything of me

Mama
Mama

Go away

Mama
Mama

Go away children
Go away day
Go away everything

LEAVE ME!

There is a depression
in my mattress
that is
me
and then I get up and take my kids to school anyway
it's a sort of mundane agony.

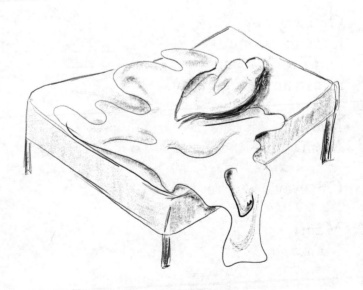

Lazy Slumber

I love this hazy
lazy
slumber
that draws down my lids
after a good cry
for no good reason
(but life)
It's like drawing the warm covers
over my head
and sleeping in
as a dawn so still
rises
after a thunderstorm.

Insomnia

Every night
I just give up
and plant my feet
and just stand up

Give up on sleep
who runs away
plays hard to get
the more you pray

I tell myself
no prob, okay
still got enough
to start the day

And here I am
coffee brewed hot
sharing my poems
and my thoughts

Yes, my insomnia
is sometimes sad
but overall
it's not that bad

Good morning :)

Friendship

I went away for a long time
I wasn't good at keeping in touch
I came home
called my friends
naively, tentatively
(are they the same? am I?
does it matter that I'm back?)

Hey... I'm back... want to catch up?
and so we met
and I was so relieved
so, so relieved
that they had saved me a seat
in their hearts
all this time
and they were the same people I'd left behind
only more...
more grown, more beautiful
and we just picked up where we left off
briefly treaded over light updates
then dove deep into the pains
that can be shared only with friends

And our tears showed me
the colour of our love:
transparent
constant
same
forever.

Forgiveness

I look at you behind bars
I turn the key in the lock
finally forgiving you
letting you go
setting you free

The door swings outward
away from me

Ha.

You were always free
I was the one behind bars

Forgiveness frees the forgiver.

Dying

He was dying
slowly
he said:

I don't know how to die
I'm not ready
I'm afraid to sleep and not wake up

He asked me to visit him
so we could talk
so I could help him
(what did I know of dying?)

He would freshen up
and eagerly wait for me
but once I came
he always fell asleep

It was like...
he relaxed just enough
to let go
knowing or hoping
I would guard him
in his sleep

Be an anchor
from this world
so he could go

to sleep
but not go
too far off
to death.

Death

I think
I think
of death
every day
it makes me feel alive
and reminds me
to live.

Grief

It comes in waves
slow waves of grief
with so very little
in-between relief

No sooner
do I catch my breath
than I get pulled under
to a kind of death

Missing you
is slowly killing me
just let me drown
or set me free

Please
just let me drown
or set me free.

Wishing Myself to Death

What is this heaviness
that warns me
not to come fully awake
but remain treading
under sleep's sweet oblivion?

I ignore it and surface anyway
you know how it is...
when you want to keep testing a sore spot
does it still hurt?
or when you want to retrieve a memory
just out of reach

The moment I rise to consciousness
I groan and wish myself back to sleep
or even to death
as the wave of longing hits me and I

again

start drowning in your memory

I had kept you distant all yesterday
but you must have gotten through
as I let my guard down and my eyes grew heavy
cruelly, you waited in my dreams
ready to be the first thought
to greet me when I woke

And here I am

again

wishing myself
back to sleep
or even to death
just to forget you.

My Dreams

I'm going to bed now
I know you are gone forever
but please
do visit me in my dreams
I miss you so.

One Day

The broken child cries
when will it stop?
when will the pain go away?

The old soul replies
it doesn't matter
you only have to
get through this day

The child sniffs
just this day?
one day?

okay.

Losing a Father

Losing a father
is like
having the earth
pulled from under you
and the roof
of your cosy home
blown off

You are
no longer
warm
safe
protected

You've lost your shoes
you walk barefoot now

You've lost your status
as:

Princess.

Betrayal

A stab in the back
a fall to the knees
excruciating pain

Can't catch my breath
my open heart
will never be the same

Slowly with time
open my eyes
to see, who hurt me, who?

No, no
eyes lie, and all my friends
no way that it was you

Tell me I'm wrong
that they betray
I'll take your word, I swear

Despite the blood
on guilty hands
your prints are everywhere

But why? why? why?
one question drums
beats on me like the rain

No answer, none
that's it, I'm done
I'll never trust again
But I will... someday.

You don't get to change who I am.

Have You Ever

Have you ever
felt
like you had no armour
no skin

The wind, when it blew
hurt
the gazes of people
when they looked at you
pierced

Your haunted eyes
betrayed you
with their glass film of tears
ever present
ever threatening
to overflow

Your mouth let you down
as every forced-up smile
died
before making it
to your quivering lips

Have you ever
felt
so naked and raw
you had to hide behind walls
and under covers

Have you?
I understand
I have too

I'm me
and I'm you.

Chapter 2
Individual

As individuals, we are each different in our own way. There is no point in being all modest about it. We'd do better to accept the miracle of our uniqueness, scary though it may be. I think we are born knowing this, then we forget somewhere along the way as we are moulded into other people's dreams and pressured to conform to other people's rules. We grow up and become ever so attuned to the world's expectations and the eyes supposedly upon us that we no longer detect our own desires—that whim to wear mismatched socks, listen to uncool music, or stay home and read if that is our pleasure. So our lives become a quest to reconnect with, and rediscover who we are.

You need to be brave when doing this, because if you're honest in your quest, you will find some inconvenient truths. You may discover you love something you cannot have, hate a tradition you feel you must keep, and wage battles within yourself as you decide which battles with others to pick. Being yourself out loud can cost you, and it can be brave. Yet there are some parts of yourself you may decide to keep hidden for the sake of others or your relationships with them. That can be very brave too.

I am on the beginning of my journey, and here are some of the things I've learned so far:

I think I'm an introvert, and that's okay. [3]
So much energy is wasted in conforming to others' expectations.
People don't like you for being nice, but for being authentic.
They respect you more for that, too.
You are allowed to be things that "don't go together".
You don't need to apologize for not fitting into a box or an image.
You don't have to apologize for being contradictory,
for reconciling irreconcilable aspects of yourself,
for being conservative yet passionate,
feminine but strong,
caring for your children yet
yearning for your freedom.

---

[3] I loved Susan Cain's book *Quiet: The Power of Introverts in a World That Can't Stop Talking* (New York: Crown Publishing, 2012), on the power of introverts.

On your journey, it helps to imagine being invisible. With no eyes upon you, how would you be? *Who* would you be? It helps to look inward for answers, not outward. It helps to systematically be curious about your tastes and values, to explore, discover, choose what you love, and free yourself of the rest.

Two of Michelangelo's quotes speak to me when I think of the process of finding oneself:

'Every block of stone has a statue inside it and it is the task of the sculptor to discover it.'

and:

'I saw the angel in the marble and carved until I set him free.'

The process of finding yourself is like finding your sculpture in a slab of rock. You become more beautiful and refined as you age because you become more authentic, more truthful, more you, without the noise and fuss.

I lost touch with myself for a long time as I scrambled to fill and understand my other roles. Under this hat of "Individual" are some of my most personal discoveries on the quest to find my way back to myself, things unique to me.

The fact that I love turquoise and horseback-riding, and that I chose medicine as a specialty may have nothing to do with you, yet I share these things with you hoping it will allow you to find out and *live out* what makes *you* special as an individual.

To unapologetically go for it,
to go ahead and just:

be yourself.

Hello

I sat
alone
and did something I had not done
in a long, long time
I said to myself:
hello
hello, Wid
Wid?
no answer
where are you?
where am I?
I sat and sat, searching
finally, I found me
huddled in a corner
in the crevices of my heart
wearing rusty rollerblades
so lonely
so young
nineteen, to be exact
hey...
I miss you
I'm sorry I haven't come to see you
or ask how you've been doing
I stroke your hair—mine
short-like a boy's,
fairy-like
(you're guarded)
I say:

I won't demand anything from you this time
I swear
I'm sorry I've pushed you so hard
can I sit with you?
visit with you?
please, I'm lost
can you remind me of what I liked to do?
it's a faint whisper
but with some hope
and I remember...
I loved to rollerblade and paint in watercolours and write
and ride horses and sit alone on the garden swing

That was my favourite place to cry
I cry now for myself
though that childhood swing
that swing my father pushed so high
that we squealed with terrified laughter
is gone
as is he

I have to go
but let's stay in touch
I won't be so hard on you anymore
I promise
remind me how to be me
with your wise innocence
forgive me
I love you
I wid you
"Wid" is an Arabic word that means
the strongest kind of love.

In Defence of Introverts
I

There is no right flavour
of coffee
or happiness
or pleasure
it's okay to enjoy staying home.

In Defence of Introverts II

One reason I hate big parties:
I'm too aware
of all the heartbeats
in the room
and I like
to listen to hearts
one
at
a
time.

In Defence of Introverts
III

Why do I need so much

Space?

To spread out the worlds
enfolded inside me.

Why do I need so much

Time?

To distil these worlds
into words
for you.

In Defence of Introverts IV

I retreat
to solitude
not because
I do not care
but because
I care
so much.

Sweet Tooth

I'm lonely so I eat
something comforting and sweet
to fill up the void
and help me avoid
my emptiness till we meet

Uh-oh...
now I'm feeling full
on the couch I need to lie
I guess I shouldn't have eaten
that second pecan pie.

A true story.

Evergreen

Some of us
are ancient
Evergreen trees
with roots that will gut the earth
if wrenched out

We are peaceful
and quite happy where we are

Call us old-fashioned
call us old
but don't
please don't
call us ignorant
naïve
simpleminded

Don't call to us
to uproot
to follow in your footsteps
at your pace

You have no right
to educate us
to save us
to enlighten us
to patronize

We are fine
we see just fine
we know what you're saying
and we're saying we're not interested

If and when
we choose to shed our leaves
or find a new way
of being in the world
it will be
of our own accord

And we hope there will still be
Evergreens
Everthere
to remind us

of where we'd been
of who we were
of who we will
Forever be.

Punk

Punky hair
in jet-stone black
spikes not falling
down my back

With undertones of
Prussian Blue
that's a look
I'd like to do

Maybe pierce my nose
maybe change my clothes

You don't believe me
but it's true

Just for a day.

Why does it threaten you
that I choose the path less travelled?
I don't compel you to walk it
so why not leave me be?

To pursue your image
as reflected in the eyes of others
is to be aimlessly
          pulled
in   every
direction
               of their
                    wandering

                         gaze.

Resident

Lub dub+
put on your scrubs
show up on your very first day

You're a resident now
so pretend you know
the items on the surgical tray

Better suck it up
better show up and smile
and practice your "no-problem" face

Better hold your ground
and never make a sound
and show no fear, not a trace

Your pager's going off
heart jamming up your throat
it's happening: your first code blue

You're it, you're on
get your act together now
someone's life is depending on you

+ In medicine, *lub* and *dub* refer to the first and second heart sounds, respectively.

One day you'll look back
wonder how you did it all
recall helping hands on the way

So please extend your own
to the next R1 you meet
when they too freak on their very first day

Congratulations for making it
you are a SUPERSTAR!
and I never doubted you for a moment :)

Dr. Captain Awesome-Pants

I was worried I wouldn't pass my exams, and a friend
said:
Don't be ridiculous! You're Wid!
You're Doctor Captain Awesome-Pants!

You know what's coming up?
my practical exam
in all of med and surgery
it's really time to cram

It's not an easy one, this one
but I think I stand a chance
if I tell myself that I will be
Doctor Captain Awesome-Pants!

It's been long since I really did
full head-to-toe exams
but I'm going to do my best that day
so here it is, my plan:

I won't say: Please call Trauma!
right now! fast as can be!
cuz who's the trauma team, Wid?
oh, shoot! I guess it's me

What types of bleeding are there?
I won't forget, I won't!

there is bleeding that you see
and bleeding that you don't

What shocks kill trauma patients?
those that obstruct and those that bleed
compress, reduce, or tourniquet
chest tubes and labs you need

Glasgow, Apgars, ABCs
I've got them to the letter
if you are bleeding on the ground
think I can make it better

Looks like appendicitis
if I have a tiny doubt
I'll call Gen Surg, my brave old friends
and they will take it out

Wid, please remember, say your name
and smile and wash your hands
explain what you are thinking
on patients' right must stand

In every case, do vitals
inspect, palpate, percuss
and auscultate and be polite
and get the patient's trust

Whatever case scenario
play *cool*, for goodness' sake
as Captain Doctor Awesome-Pants
this quiz? a piece of cake.

Who Are "THEY"?

Please, someone tell me
enlighten me
please explain to me
who are They?

And why do we all
care so much
about
what they will say?

Do they sit
in mighty towers
write rules
all night and day?

Who selected them?
who put them on
the committee anyway?

Come here
come close
a secret
I'll tell you who they are

They're me and you
backstabbers too
this joke has gone too far

By following
their silly rules
you'll never be the star

Just do your thing
just find your way
and just be:

who you are.

Live your life in a way
that allows you to be fearless
in the face of death

No regrets.

Vacations give us the chance
to temporarily escape
be someone else
who is somehow
more like ourselves.

A

I've always been an A
though I love the letter B
fewer edges, softer curves
and closer to the C

Sure, As are full of drive
aggression to succeed
but Bs are so relaxed
at their not-so-breakneck speed

As climb up and up and up
to reach the lonely top
where Bs will smell the roses
laze around, just breathe, and stop

It's true that in the end
As make a lot of money
but Bs build hives and lives
Bs make our homes
and honey.

Wasting a Day

Before leaving Montreal...

Wasting a day
Paris Crepe Café
and maybe a show of
Cirque du Soleil
Cavalia, horse riding
shopping at la Bai
a couple of movies
and a last ballet

That's my "perhaps list"
for the rest of my stay
but today... is for resting
it's my wasting-time day.

May

My birthday's coming up this May
I'd like a jellyfish
or a mermaid tail
or fairy wings
it never hurts to wish

Or a unicorn or a pegasus
or hair as blue as seas
of shimmering waves
a waterfall
that tumbles to the knees

Although I'm shy, I'll tell you
these are my favourite things
I'd be happy with a birthday wish
whatever friendship brings

My favourite flowers
are peonies
of the softest
pinkish white

My food
is peanut butter
I'll savour
every bite

My colour
is turquoise green
for my sore eyes
such a sight

My time of day
is dawn
just at the break
of light

My city
is Madina
home to
the prophet's flight

I doubt that you'll remember
but I'm hoping that you might
send me a thought
or gift, or wish
since I've helped you get it right.

My Face

I look in the mirror
squint
frown
try to catch my profile

I decide that
my face
may not be
a face to be admired
but it's one that
has character
and it's one that
can be trusted

I'm grateful.

Some grow better
when left alone.
See you when I'm ready.

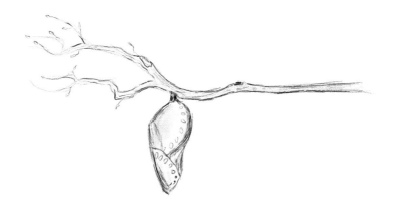

It's so liberating
to realise
you can just be you
as you are
as you are
as you are.

Deep down inside
you know you are great
stop the drama
the false modesty
and own it.

To be seen for who you are
is somehow at once
our deepest fear
and our greatest desire.

Chapter 3
Writer

A long time ago, before I could type or reach for high shelves, I saw a card in my favourite bookstore in Riyadh. "Jarir" it was called. The card's title read, "One day you'll write a book." I thought of buying it for myself but felt that was pretentious and ridiculous. I tucked my wish away. Months later, my father gave me that card, so I read it and let myself dream. It was about how I, the receiver of this card, was in fact a dreamer, a people-watcher, a girl who finds shapes in the clouds of the sky. It talked about how one day I would write a book.

I wrote my first story when I was in first grade. It was six pages long and titled *Little Lemony*. I spent my summers writing and illustrating in my spare copy books. But writing a book? That idea gathered dust with my precious card.

Until now.

Now I wear a writer's hat, and I'm a real writer. As you may be too. When I posted my first quote on Instagram, I thought: Who am I to come up with quotes, to share wisdom? Well, with a gulp, I ask: who am I *not to*?

Writing is not about publishing. It's about how you see the world, feel it, process it, put words to experiences, capture beauty and sorrow in a phrase. Or a quote. Or a tweet. If you keep a journal, have a private blog, or write poetry, you're already a writer with a writer's hat of your own, and I am so happy to meet you.

Buried

I've come to accept that I'll die
with so many books—and children
yet inside me
never to see light of day
never once meant to stay
not to be left for the world
behind me

I'm content that I've one
and another I've begun
that much at least, is not
denied me

Those inside me still
I will love as well
and hold close
when buried with me
inside me.

Real

I am a real writer
because on occasion
I name something
in other people's hearts
so that they feel
more understood
less alone
and that's real enough for me.

Words

I am so grateful for
thick books
and inky pens
and sharpened pencils
and unlined journals

and for words
I am so grateful for words.

Between

All I want to say
is what you want to say
I just want to
put words
to your pain
and heartaches
and headaches
and bittersweet moments
they are all mine too, you see

And if we could just
together
somehow
distil the tears
into words
held in this
space/screen/glance/page
between us

then there's this hope
that maybe our pain
will be divided
between us

become more
bearable
and maybe
a little beautiful

for bringing us
a few words
and a whole world
closer.

Moving is profoundly
moving.

There is a difference between
looking at someone
and really seeing them.

It's hard
to grow roots
when you're standing in quicksand.

Forget the positive, "you-can-do-it" hype
sometimes it really is
not you
sometimes it really is
the environment
or life
give yourself a break
you're still standing, aren't you?

I am here again
on this too-familiar
well-trodden path
of memories
yesterday's footprints
mine
still fresh on the ground
I think it's a circular path
I think I'm stuck
I think I'm lost.

Careful how you break the news
or you might just
break the person.

I was an idiot.
No, you were an innocent.
There is no shame in being more beautiful
than the world deserves.

The flower we all long to be:
Forget-me-not.

We often choose to forget
the most unforgettable things.

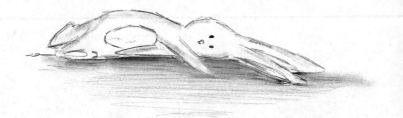

Omar

Sometimes your reality
is all that matters
the fact that the stars
you gaze upon tonight
may have died light years ago
does not take away
from the beauty of your night
or the fact that
they give you direction
and light.

Let the hands of time
pass over your wounds
and heal you.

Lying by omission
is the most hurtful of lies
it allows the liar
to lie
about their lying.

Things
Take
Time.

Each time
could be your last time
so make it last.

You can't change other people
but you can change
the steps to your dance
or choose
to stop dancing
altogether.

Live
and risk everything
or hide
and risk not living.

Some people talk so much
but don't really say anything
while others can carry a silence
that says everything.

It's impossible to see
the whole picture
when you're

smack

in the middle of it.

Acknowledge your pain
but don't befriend it.

If what needs to be said between us
is unspeakable
then let's at least respect it
with a sacred silence
unpeppered with lies
and pointless small talk.

The time you give to yourself
is an investment
not a waste.

Future happiness is a mirage
don't die of thirst chasing it
forgetting to gratefully sip
from the water bottle
you hold in your two hands
right now.

Don't try to make all your fantasies come true
save some for your dreamland
let them live on there
enjoy their forbidden distance
their impossibility.

If your hands are shaking with rage
as you type
hit Save
not Send.

Sleep on it.

You cannot build a dam in the midst of a flood
all you can do is
stay afloat
stay alive
survive
then maybe
maybe you can channel the raging waters
into something less destructive
or even
poignantly beautiful.

You miss your past, I know
but if you visit it too often
you'll miss your present, too

Let go of all the feelings about THE feeling
they only make it worse.

Writing is
therapy
for the soul.

Lost

What is truly lost
is not what you remember and miss
it's what you've forgotten
or worse—never lived
as it happened
it's what you missed.

Decide

One foot
on either side
of the great divide
that is gaping
ever wide
I must decide:
which side?
for to hesitate
is to fall through
to hesitate
is suicide.

Allow yourself the gift
of seeing yourself
as others see you.

Light is more meaningful
to those who know darkness.

Chapter 4
Woman

There are things only a woman can know, things about the way our minds and bodies and hearts work, and there are experiences only we will encounter. I see this every day in my own life and in my practice as a women's mental-health psychiatrist and life coach.

Dear men, we love you and need you, but please take a moment to reflect on this: Listen. *Listen.* Most of history, literature, art, even medicine for that matter was studied, and written and conducted from a masculine point of view, as women held the homes and forts—invisible soldiers. We have not had the opportunity to voice our views and experiences until recently—and our voice is still limited. I want you to look at us not as pretty roses and precious gems. Those are *objects*. We are *people*. We are souls, human beings whose bodies happen to take this feminine form. This will be easier for you to grasp if you have a daughter. Look at her. *See* her.

When we wear our women's hats, entirely different meanings are given to femininity, feminism, strength, soft power, love, caregiving, independence, and sisterhood. In some cultures, womanhood is too closely tied to motherhood. I have come to see them as possibly overlapping, but mostly separate. Womanhood does not need motherhood to complete it. Funnily enough, becoming a mother had steered me away from feeling like a woman for a long time. I was too busy taking care of others to experience myself as a woman. Then I had my daughter, who lives her life unaware, as I watch her in awe and learn lessons of self-love and unapologetic self-admiration, and remember the pleasures of dressing up in glitter and feathers. She reminds me of how to be my own kind of woman.

This chapter is relatively short, partly because I am still exploring what womanhood means to me and partly, I admit, because I'm weary of offending, of being the "wrong kind" of feminist. For reasons I'm still trying to figure out, women don't give each other enough of a break, though if we empathized with each other more, mentored one another more, and judged each other less, we might heal the world, one woman at a time.

Not only can a woman
make a home
but she can be her own home
her own temple
her own contented universe
even as
she stands alone.

Woman

Woman
Wonder
Wonderful
Willow tree
Wavy hair
Water
Waiting
Wallflower
Waistline
What
Would this
World be
Without
Women?

She woke up early
stretched her
fleece-pyjama-covered body
brewed her coffee
in fuzzy slippers
and looked forward to the company
she had planned for this day

From shopping
to the spa
to lounging at home
she had so many appointments booked
and so looked forward to spending time with:
herself.

Her father
never saw her
when she was little
so she spent her youth
searching
for her reflection
in the eyes
of every man.

Her Own

She holds a degree
She holds a job
She holds their hearts
She holds her own
She owns herself.

Dear daughter,
you don't always
have to be
a good girl

Stay feisty and strong
change what you see wrong
don't be afraid to fight
when fighting is right

What can I say?
sometimes being a good girl
means being
as bad
as a bad boy

but fiercer.

Turquoise

I'm no one's pink silhouette
tired of society's etiquette
I have a name and a face
I have a voice, yeah, you bet

I'm going to walk tall again
going to wear my turquoise blue
I couldn't care any less
if it's a shade too bright for you

See, I've tried to conform
tried to curtsy, smile, and twirl
but I have to stand up for me
and more so for my baby girl

For she will do as I do
kids never do as you say
and I'll teach her to be true
to her true colours all the way

Mimi, I'm so excited for you to find your own
turquoise
Love, Mama.

Arrow

Let me tell you something
about me
about the type of woman
who stands before you
I'm a straight-arrow one
a no-nonsense one
a loyal one—to the bone

Don't take my kindness
for seduction
nor my smile
as invitation
if you make that mistake
your loss

You'll lose
what I was willing to offer for free—
not my body
something much more valuable to you
if only you knew

I'd have given you
light and wisdom and warmth and safety
and a rare kindness
I'd have taught you all I know

All you had to do
was show some respect
for my boundaries
for my values
for who I am.

Honourable

It is honourable
to be the woman
behind the man
the one who raises men
and feeds them
and cheers them on
and tends their wounds
when they come back broken

It is also honourable
to be the woman
in the arena.

Free

Unlike
the precious objects
you collect
those you display
out there
for all to see

Unlike
the other ones
the ones you hide
the ones you guard
with jealousy

I'm not your object
I belong to me
to "keep" me
is to leave me free

For the surest way
to lose me
is to try
—just try
to lock me up
and hide the key

You see?

How Dare You

How dare you
raise your hand to me!
how dare you
touch a hair

On my coiffed head!
my hairdo!
do you think
that I am scared?

You say
you didn't mean it
you say it
like I care

The first time
is the hardest
so you'll surely
again dare

You lost me
before it landed
your fist
still in mid-air

You touched me once
that was our end
touch me again
you'll end, I swear

And do you know how much I paid to get my hair done?
Stupid bully.

To be a woman
is to be a caregiver
it's just that
we forget
to give care
to ourselves.

Blind to Beauty

I see
so many beautiful women
who don't see
their own beauty
it drives me crazy
there's this particularly
frustrating case
whom I see
every single day
in the mirror.

She died beautiful
at the young age of thirty-three
only a single faint line furrowed her brows
she used to worry about aging, you see
all that worry
for nothing.

Gentlemen, a Few Tips:

For many of us
you'll have to guess
what's truly
on our minds

Don't be so sure
the times we say
go out, have fun
it's fine

And when you ask:
are you okay?
please ask
at least three times

Put your screens away
look into our eyes
dress up for us
be kind

We want to know
you care enough
to know
what lies behind

Our words and smiles
and will you stay
after finding
what you find?

Dear Sister

Don't give yourself away
don't hide yourself away

but it's okay
to sometimes
run away
or get carried away

in order to ultimately
find your way
or make your way.

Grooming

It's true
that we groom
to seduce, sometimes
but mostly
it's for ourselves
and every so often
it's for Battle.

Circle

Nothing is stronger
than a circle of women
holding hands.

Let's not compete
in uncomfortable heels
but dance
barefoot
to the top
together.

Ladies
stop judging each other
and, more importantly
stop trying to "save" each other

Gentlemen
just stay out of it
this is not about you.

Not every woman
wants or needs
a man
or a child
to feel complete

She is strong enough
to stand alone
she is wise enough
to know
she is already
whole.

Dressing Up

I used to love
being fancy
as a girl

To dress up
in all those pearls
and twirl

Glitter
feathers
fans that
unfurl

The natural
dressing up
of girls.

Dressing Down

Then I grew up
became aware

Of how the men
around would stare

It seemed
a man's world
out there

Had to
dress it down
to get anywhere.

Now

Now I'm growing back
to that little girl
dress up or down
without a care

Too pretty
too plain
too covered
too bare

Take a long look
at my face—
does it look
like I care?

(anymore)

W

Women
Would heal the
World
Without
War

When
We
Work together
We
Work
Wonders.

There is *nothing*
you can do
to become
more beautiful

Well, maybe one thing:
you could add that sparkle to your eyes
that comes from *knowing*
you are beautiful.

Real Face

Her frown lines
spelled compassion
her crow's feet
always smiled
her grey hair
reflected the light
and her wisdom

Such beauty
in her real face
it was a face to trust
and come home to.

Chapter 5
Mother

The hat of "mother" is too big for me and is forever falling off my head. I'm growing into it and sometimes want to shout, 'I'm doing my best, everyone, so please give me a break!' Nothing really prepares us for motherhood; it's not all bliss and roses, and I wish the world and the mothers in it would stop pretending it was.

Let me tell you a secret I learned from my own experience and from working in the women's mental-health field: all mothers find motherhood difficult at times. We all have dark moments, and we all long to be alone, to escape, and to distance ourselves from our children at times. From what type of milk we give our children to what master's degree we encourage them to pursue, I think we are so afraid of messing this job up, so insecure about our parenting that we—mothers—shame each other to assure ourselves that even if we're doing a bad job as mothers, at least someone else is making a bigger mess of motherhood.

Stop. Everyone. Relax. Do your best and leave the rest. We are all in this together.

The best parenting book I have ever read is actually not a parenting book. It's a chapter from *Daring Greatly* [5] by Brené Brown which speaks to children's need to have a sense of worthiness and belonging. And you cannot give what you do not have; in order for our children to feel these things, we, as parents, need to feel them first. She also emphasizes that as parents, the best we can do is be engaged with our children, and simply *pay attention*. The chapter is a comforting reminder that as parents we are all largely working things through as we go along.

I want to take a moment to point out that there are invisible mothers who don't have babies in their arms. They never had the chance to, or are unable to conceive their babies, or carry them to term. Or they carried them, then lost them. They are still mothers. They may be the bravest truest mothers. I acknowledge and honour them.

---

[5] Brown, Brené. "Chapter 7." In *Daring Greatly*.

And then, there are fathers. I know you feel a lot of what we feel, and maybe more. This chapter is for you, too. I honour you as well.

In this chapter, I try to retrace some of my own mother's footsteps. I find I sometimes follow her lead and sometimes try to forge a new path. I often circle back to where she must have stood. The more I wade into the waters of motherhood, the more I appreciate her sacrifices, the more I love her—in retrospect—and the more I feel the need to say: thank you.

I'll leave you now with these words that touch on the joys and woes of motherhood, how we are changed when we love little boys and girls, the million ways in which our children teach us, and so much more.

I'm trying
to grow up
fast
in time
to raise my children
before
they are all

          grown up.

Apparently,
there is a word
to describe
the rapid growth
hormonal changes
mood swings
and turbulence

To describe
the time when
someone's body is changing
so that they're clumsy
and uncomfortable

The time when
a person
is growing so fast
propelled into adulthood
and responsibility
before they're quite ready

Introducing not:
Adolescence
but:
Matrescence[6]
such comfort in putting a name to "it"
so that "it" becomes normal.

---

[6] Matrescence is a term coined by Dana Raphael, and re-introduced by Alexandra Sack, *"A New Way to Think About the Transition to Motherhood."* TED Talk. May 2018.

When I held you
in my arms
that very first time

I was filled with hope
and love

Your innocence
made me believe again
in fresh starts
and new beginnings.

Mothering is like fathering—
you do it
but it does not become
all of who you are.

Sticky Situation

(Read in the Voice of Omar, Aged Five)

Sticky situation
beyond imagination
involving Mom's turquoise goo

Silly magic putty
really wasn't funny
sticking to my hair like glue

Don't sleep with it at night
don't let the bedbugs bite
Dad told me, but I didn't hear

Woke up with putty in my hair
blue and furry like a bear
A vision to instil some fear

I started to cry
but knew it was okay
when I saw my mom's laughing eyes

We'll get it out, don't worry
although we have to hurry
we'll be late to school, but let's try

One day, you'll laugh about this
she said as she removed
one sticky blue piece at a time

And even as she did
I saw that it *was* funny
and together
we made this poem rhyme.

Dimples

Playful dimples
that seem to wink
a smile of
dappled sunlight
so bright you blink

Downy soft skin
as smooth as mink
gold bangles that dance
with a tinkly tink

I love you, baby girl
much more than you think
so there it is, written
in stone and in ink.

Mother of Boys

I'm used to messy rooms
and floors scattered with toys
used to stickers on walls
and the clatter of noise

I know all about paintings
done in blues and turquoise
about blocks tumbling down
with one slam that destroys

About ice cream and rainbows
and a million small joys
that make life so full
see, I'm a mother
of boys.

Dear Daughter

The world
will sometimes say to you
you have to choose between

Glitter and muscle
heels and power
no one likes a too-powerful Queen

Well, here's a secret
I hope you won't keep
you're entitled to be you
and to dream

To be both torn jeans
and soft pink velveteen
to be both rough edges
and glimmering sheen

To oppocontrarily
make up words and define
what being
a strong woman means.

Dear Mimi

A Letter to You on Your First Birthday

At the tender age of one, you are wiser than I am in ways, and you have taught me a lot.

You look into the mirror, and you laugh, delighted with your reflection. You know you are beautiful, and most girls, including me, forget.
Don't forget.

When your father or brothers enter the room, you give them that "What are you all waiting for?" look. You demand to be picked up, to be carried. And so many girls have given up on being "carried" despite being perfectly able to walk. So many girls have forgotten their value.
Don't forget.

Having you is transforming me. I know you will do as I do and not as I say. I've always worked hard at being a better mother, but for you, I'm working on being a better woman.

I love you.
Don't forget.

Love,
Mama.

Cosy Rain

(Read in the Voice of Abdulrahman, Aged Nine)

Mama! I'm:

Soaking wet
pouring rain
plastered hair
such a pain

Not exactly
where I want to be
get me home right now
fast as can be

Click, stomp, squelch, slam, sigh, finally!

Cosy cabin
crackling fire
warm pyjamas
just out of the dryer

My favourite book
hot cocoa so sweet
looking through the window
at the puddly street

It's comforting now
that patter of rain
soothing, cosy, nice
not at all a pain.

Crossing Guard

Every day you stand
help them cross the busy street
bring them safely to the shore
on their busy kid feet

Back and forth you walk
retrace your steps for miles
across the intersection
always sending out your smiles

Smiles that reach your laughing eyes
and brighten up their days
and ease our parent minds
in many, many ways

Thank you!

Abdul

If the world
had your heart, Abdul
what a place it would be...
so cool

You, who cried
when you knew
the Tasmanian tiger
was extinct before you
before you were even born

But you cried for it
soaked your pillow
'Why? why did they kill them all?
They weren't dangerous! They didn't do anything!'

You who asked me once
with your hands on your shaking head
how do people do this?
how do you steal something?
how do you *kill someone*?
how?!

You who wave at strangers and say:
See, Mama
it's a game...
you wave and see who waves back
and people always wave back to you, my love

If only the world had your heart, Abdul
what a place it would be
Paradise.

Me Time

I love my me time
my I-am-free time
my I-can-see time
so crystal-clear time

I love to be alone
my soul is my real home
the lone queen on her throne
the silence etched in stone

I love my cosy space
my mind in outer space
my heart the only pace
it's inwards that I face

Call me a selfish mom
to steal some time at dawn
but it's my salve, my balm
me time's my peace and calm

It's how I figure out
what my whole life's about
when I silence all my doubts
when I scream out and shout:

I'm still heeeeeeeeeeeeeeeeeeeeeeeeeeeere!

Honestly, you should try it out.

When?

Baby
when did you pass away?
was I laughing?
was I fast asleep?
I wish I knew the moment
to go back to it
and weep

When they said
your heart gave way
I was sure mine would stop as well
I could swear
I still felt you kicking
in my now-familiar swell

It's funny
how my heart still beats
though I don't know whatever for
if my life is gone: you
then I'm not sure
what I live for anymore.

Growing into Motherhood

Motherhood
was a cosy, loose red sweater
that was just too big for me
the sleeves were too long
I couldn't hold all I needed to hold
I kept dropping things
and tripping over the dragging hem

I wanted to take it off
to be me again
to be pretty again
to be free again
untethered

But you held on, little one
not caring about my flaws
my tousled hair
my fluffy skin
my double chin

You had eyes only for me
you looked up so adoringly
in your eyes
I could do no wrong

So for your puppy-brown eyes
I rolled up my sleeves
and grew strong
and grew into this motherhood sweater
until it fit perfectly—almost

It became my skin
which you breathe in
day out and day in.

Upside Down

One boy says to his brother:
Hey, Moony, Moony, look!
I'm gonna do something
that will make Mama gasp like this:
ahhhhhhhh!

Sigh...
what's with my boys
and upside down?
I get it's smiles
and no more frowns

Only thing is
my mother's heart
which somersaults
until they're down

Can't they just stand
like normal kids
with both feet firmly
on the ground?!

Must they swing so high
while standing up
and must they land
with such a sound?

Can't they just slide
from up to down
instead of climbing
all around?

Can't they have mercy
on this heart
know that their risks
will make it pound?

I swear I age
at least ten years
with every trip

to our playing ground.

The Baby Cries

The baby cries
her heart rate
accelerates
overwhelming panic
then decelerates
sinking dread

The baby cries
and his cries
are the fingers
that strum the guitar strings
of her heart

But it's not a happy tune
it's sad and angry and guilty and terrifying
mixed with love
that is hard to find
to feel
amidst the hopelessness
and the helplessness

The baby cries again—or still
she wants to scream so loud
to drown it out
instead, she goes to him
and cradles him
and hides her shame
and wonders
what's wrong with me?

Sick Only

My dearest wish
this evening
is to be sick only
just sick

Without the guilt of being
a sick mother
without the harsh, innocent
un-understanding, unforgiving accusing
glares of my child

You never play with me anymore!
You always sleep!
I hate you!
I won't hug you forever!

Please
have mercy
stop
I hate myself enough
for failing you
my love

Please stop
your five-year-old words
eat at me
more than this illness

I just want
to be sick
sick only
what a luxury
that would be.

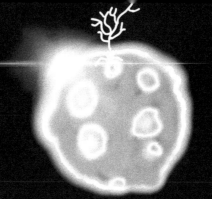

moony

Don't orbit around your children
you are a world unto yourself
a Universe
with her own trajectory
and moons and dreams of her own.

Don't live for your children
Live *with* them.

Being a mother
should never stop you
from being yourself.

Perfection is the enemy
of parenting.

Our children are not
our sculptures
to be moulded
not our stories
to be told
not the vessels
for our unfinished dreams

They are seeds
with their own life force
to be cultivated

Give them the basic elements
sun
and water
and love
and a place to grow roots

Then step back
let them grow
and be delightedly surprised
by the colours of their bloom.

A Mother's Scent

(Read in the Voice of Omar, Aged Five)

Mama, if I smell you and smell you and smell you
will your smell finish?

Kids
I'm sorry you got stuck with
this kind of mother:
the human kind.

Thank you, little one
for making me a mother
for showing me
what happens
when you give yourself
for a while, at least
give yourself over
fully
to another.

Chapter 6
Romantic

I envision the "romantic" hat, more like a mask. I guess it's because our romantic sides are often private, and it feels easier to be brave with our hearts from behind a mask and some armour. I'm shy and conservative by nature. I grew up in a conservative environment and admit that I often have to ask my clients to fill me in on things that are not obvious to me when they tell me of their courting, dating, or romantic lives.

I am not a romantic adventurer, but I have two superpowers: empathy and imagination. With empathy and imagination, I can go anywhere, walk in anyone's shoes, and feel—to a degree at least—what their hearts feel. I read romantic novels and cry at the end when the hero dies. I listen to others and get swept up in their tales of love. I see couples on the street and make up all sorts of stories about them (in my head, of course). I notice when the young groom plays with his bride's hair and when the old man fills up his wife's plate, gently spreading the sauce evenly over her rice, just the way she likes it, just the way he has done for the past forty-three years.

I believe in love and heartbreak as real and powerful experiences that can shape our lives and who we are. Through my roles as therapist, confidante, and coach, I am lucky to hear many stories, cradle many broken hearts, and sometimes even bring people together to their happy endings.

"Wid" is one of the many Arabic words for love, and as Arabs, we choose our names carefully. For us, there is a meaning or story behind every name. They say every person will manifest their name. So, Wid: Love. I love, and I enjoy writing about love. When someone tells me their story, I try to take their mess of a heartbreak and mould the shattered pieces into art and poetry. Then I gift it back to them. In this way, they, or you, may begin to see the bittersweet beauty of your own story and the sheer strength of your own character, the way I so clearly do.

Unbreakable

I am whole
unbreakable
resilient

I am so strong that
I can stand alone
I am so strong that
I can
for my pleasure
take the risk
of leaning on you

If you walk away
yes, I will fall
surprised by your betrayal
but that's on you
your flaw
not mine

If you drop me
our bond will break
but I won't break
I'll dust you off
and I'll stand tall again
eventually

Alone again
the freedom!
the sweet memories of me
before the sacrifice!

Then, if I find someone deserving
someone who can appreciate
what stands before them
someone who is in awe of me
someone who can leave me in awe
in love

I might again
for my pleasure
risk leaning
risk falling
again.

Thrill of the Chase

A man fell in love with a woman
who had no space for him
her life was already so full

He pursued and pursued
she fell
and her kind heart
made room for his loneliness

But

That room she prepared for him
that soft, downy bed
with a hundred-count thread
it became
an achingly dead space

Game on her
he just wanted
the thrill of the chase.

Burning

Holding on to his love
and keeping it inside
was like closing his fist
over burning embers

He needed to let it go
throw it into her waters
to cool

But he was afraid
she wasn't ready
to catch it

Afraid she'd burn
with his fire
so he held it in
and consumed with his passion
he burned instead.

Freezing

He never knew
that she wondered
and waited
and waited
and wondered

And in the end
died of cold
in the ice storm
of his
distance.

Two Halves

This same moon
shines upon us
both you and I

That thought
makes me smile...
that thought
makes me cry

As it waxes and wanes
and the months come and go
as the sky rains and rains
and then starts to snow

As the snow melts
gives way
to the flowers of spring
as the blooms come to life
and the birds start to sing

And the earth makes its way
'round the vast, golden sun
to the day that we met
the day life had begun

And yet still
there's no trace
of you under the sun
and yet still
we are broken

two halves

of one.

Spacetime

Every song
seems to be about you
every place feels
like a corner
where you might have stood

I retrace your steps
try to meet your eyes
by resting mine
where yours
might have looked

Wish I could trace
the world's maps
and bend spacetime...
perhaps

Day by day
across the miles and years
to find a time
and place

That might have given
our love
a chance
and some breathing space

if only, if only, if only, if only

But it just wasn't
meant to be.

On a Shelf

It's a strange feeling
for my heart
to be so awake
alive but no longer
within
myself

You have it, I think
but I feel it sink
cuz you've left it
somewhere
on a shelf.

Broken Wings

With every letter
she caught her breath
every word
made her heart
sing

Flew with every verse
of his song of love
as he spoke
unspeakable
things

She soared
till she learned
his words
weren't for her
she'd been pulled along
on a string

She crashed hard
on the harsh rocks
of the merciless truth

A pile
of broken
wings.

Lost

I've lost my heart
I can't tell where it is
it's so distant
it's wherever

you may be

Please tend to it now
unbreak it somehow
or at least

give it back to me.

Heart Be Nimble

Heart be nimble
heart be quick
heart don't break
heart don't be tricked

Be ever so careful
heed all the above
they say all is fair
in war and in love

Don't slip, don't trip
and most important of all:
whatever you do, please
please

don't fall.

Loving You

If my place in the path of your life
was meant to be
just a twig to redirect you

or a tree
to give you shade
or a softness for your head to rest

or a pile of leaves
to cushion your fall
or a breeze
to ease the heat
or a drizzle of rain
to wash away your thirst

Then so be it
I'll happily be crushed beneath you
lonely above you
and blown away
happy to evaporate
to cool your skin
even for just a little while

Let me love you
let me ease your journey
even as you never know me
even as I disappear.

True Love

Love is a verb
to do every day
it's bread-winning
it's bed-making
it's in the very mundane

It's the everyday tasks
of living and strain
it's choosing your lover
again and again

It's watering and tending
it's choosing to stay
it's seeing her beauty
in her tears and her pain

It's stoking the fires
when the fireworks fade
it's the light and warmth
in the darkness and shade

It's patience and kindness
and teaching and growing
it's pretending you don't know
despite your well-knowing

It's saying yes
to your lover
saying no
to all others

It's the beat
of a heart:
it's the rhythm
of forever.

I'm in the business of taking care of people
but you take care of me.

Dragon

My anger at you
Is a sleeping dragon
That I keep drugging
With patience
Compassion
And your empty promises
I'm so afraid to miss a dose
To let her stir or shift
Or surface into waking
Because if unleashed
Her fire will burn us both
And that might be
The end
Of
Us.

It hurts right here
in the middle
of the chest
a little to the left
over the scar you left
when you left.

Sometimes
the heart beats so fast
that it beats
the mind.

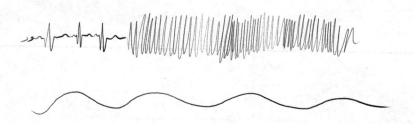

When my hand reached out to help you
it wasn't empty
it held my heart
I think that's what saved you
and what got me hurt.

He could not cross the miles between them
yet she managed to cross his mind
a thousand times a day.

The heart can beat
with a love that is true
for an image that is false

True or false?

I love you
because you are
of the numbered few
who can make me laugh
until I cry.

Love Drowned

Two lovers
on two ships
just passing through the night

Eyes met
in recognition
love like a beam of light

Their fingertips
reached out
but couldn't even brush

Across the waters
silence
hearts beating in the hush

He flung a bottle
with a letter
but that she never knew

As he never saw
and never knew
that she had flung one too

This world
was too cold, too cruel
to give them common ground

So each lived
in search of love
love lost
and true love drowned.

The phantom heart
is like
the phantom limb

It continues to hurt
long after
it is

lost.

Six Hundred Love Letters

Six hundred love letters
I sent on the wings of birds

For you
but not *to* you
I just had to
send them
away

They had to leave me
but could not reach you
they had
no place
to stay

I hope they're read
by kindred eyes
who'll send a prayer
our way.

Ghosting

Ghosting loves
disappearing acts
gone in a whiff of smoke

She holds back tears
that clog her throat
feels like she's going to choke

Again?!
Again?!
A broken heart?
Her love life was a joke

But hope...
it springs eternal
next love, a luck of stroke

Please!

Diamond Heart

I thought
I was broken forever
my heart lost and ruined and gone

But that was before knowing
my own strength
and then it dawned

My heart was not
of glass or stone
but something
ever more strong

A brilliant, blinding diamond
that shines more
when cut or wronged

Good to know.

Castle Walls

I'm sorry for always hiding
within my castle walls

Peering down at you at sunset
just when your true love calls

I think I really had to break
for you to break my fall

And waiting
you caught me home
broken wings and heart and all.

Heart!
Be still
Don't beat
Don't beat
Don't beat

yourself
to death.

The arms of a man:
Safety

The arms of a woman:
Home.

They never taught us
in med school
or in psychiatry, for that matter
why
when a heart is broken
it actually hurts
right there
where the heart is

They don't say
why
it's hard to breathe
why your chest feels
so tight
like something crushed
or so hollow
like a void
a vacant, empty space
a black hole that sucks the life
out of the rest of you

They don't have a medical name for it
or acknowledge it
as a crush injury
they don't have a treatment

Heartbreak:
this most universal
most painful
of ailments
has no name
no medicine

Just survive it.[7]

---

[7] Heartbreak is different from broken-heart syndrome, which is actually a medical term. For more on broken-heart syndrome, see "Broken Heart Syndrome." Mayo Clinic. Accessed April 2, 2019.
https://www.mayoclinic.org/diseases-conditions/broken-heart-syndrome/symptoms-causes/syc-20354617.

Waiting

He was tired
of all the girls' looks
all wanting what he had built
for himself
and for Her

But where was She?
His One?
Was he afraid to settle?
Was he afraid to commit?

No
He had a love so great
burning inside him
but only for Her

But where was She?
How long would he wait to find her?
How could he miss
a woman
he had never met?
Miss her
till his fingertips ached

Girls looked at him
he looked away
talked to them
with his head bowed
minimal side glances
as he rubbed his neck
he didn't want
to deal with them all

Only Her
Where was She?!
He'd wait.

Invisible

She was right there
but dared not say a word
she didn't look
like he expected

She couldn't compete with the false
butterfly-lashed, hair-extensioned, pouty-lipped
girls swarming him

But
she loved him
anciently
the boy he used to be
the old man he would become
the strength and beauty in between

She did not want him
to give her anything
not even to love her

If only
he would just let her
love him

And smooth that frown
as he paced
and waited
for his Her
For Her

But she dared not say a word
she did not look like he expected

She'd wait.

With one look
the earth
below her feet (and his)
shuddered
tectonic plates
shifting dangerously
an earthquake

Then a fall
into the fire.

You cannot love her
in the dark only

You cannot love her
under the curtains
of the night
if you won't love her
in the sun, in the open
in the broad day of light

You cannot love her
if you won't carry her
on your arm
if you won't
say her name
for all the world to hear

You cannot love
her body only

You must love
her mind and heart and soul
you must love her always
you must love her whole

If you won't
then please

just don't.

Calligraphy

I type your name
erase it
write it in pen
then trace it

The spelling:
an obsession
the calligraphy:

my confession.

Broken

I thought you broke me
and you did
You broke me open

And these pearls
spilling out
are just
the beginning.

Chapter 7
Muslim

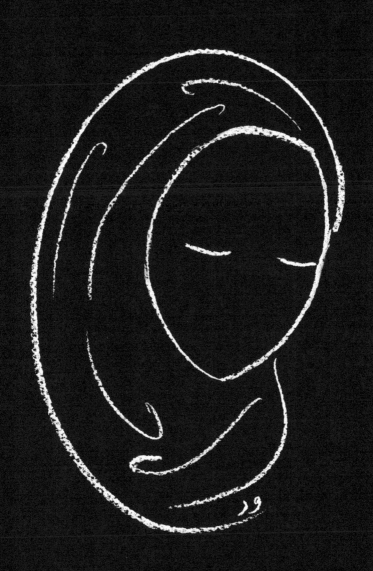

The "Muslim" hat (or veil) may be the most noticeable of my hats to anyone who meets me for the first time. It seems to be how the world today insists on defining me. Yet to me, my headscarf is a piece of clothing I use to cover a part of my body I consider private. Not every Muslim woman chooses to dress modestly or cover her hair. Not *only* Muslim women choose to dress modestly or cover their hair. Some nuns do. Some Orthodox Jewish women do.

I choose to wear the veil. It's a choice and a decision, and who is to decide that for a woman? Can you deny the beauty of a woman's hair? Of the curve of her throat? Of the line of her neck? Can you deny her right to choose what to cover and what to reveal?

When I was in Canada, there was a time when certain parties wanted to treat the veil as a religious "symbol" and ban it in public places. It was quite disturbing. I was faced with the choice of quitting my residency training or feeling like I was naked, stripped of an essential piece of clothing. *A piece of clothing*. Not a symbol, no more a symbol than your pants.

It was difficult for me to be defined by the way I was dressed. In one-off encounters, people ranged from being friendly to snobbish to openly hostile. When I had time with anyone, though—a patient, a colleague, a student—that's when I had a chance to connect with them at a deeper level, and I could *feel* the shift, in their eyes, their stance, their warmth, as if a barrier had literally fallen away and they could see me for the first time. So exhausting; so gratifying.

The veil is so visible that its value and meaning becomes overshadowed. Its value is in my being a Muslim, and being a Muslim is so much more than a way of dressing. This hat represents my spirituality, my faith, my relationship with God—my most significant relationship. I am willing to forsake all others if need be, but not this one ever-present, ever-constant, immortal, forever relationship. In that sense, this veil is my most important hat. When my hats are all in conflict and lopsided, I align them according to this one. It's the one I live for, yet the one someone might kill me for just because I choose to keep it firmly on my head and wrapped around my heart.

The poems here may come across as angry or defensive sometimes because I, as a Muslim, often feel under attack, on trial, in a position of explaining, denying, condemning, appeasing. I am not angry with you, dear reader. My anger is my prickly, puffed-up porcupine cloak. I need it to feel safe sometimes. Underneath is a lot of fear and hurt. Sometimes my arms just won't budge from their shielding position in front of my face, no matter how much I demand that they lower... lower... lower. I have the choice here to sugar-coat these feelings and soften them or share how I feel. I choose the latter, which in a way is taking a risk with you and laying down my armour, my prickly porcupine cloak.

Although you may not wear a veil, you may wear a similar hat. This hat or chapter is for every spiritual person, every visible minority, everyone who is judged at a distance, everyone who is misunderstood. It's not the shape of this hat that matters, it's the meaning.

So I'm hoping
that this most apparently distancing
of hats
might be the one that bridges
our distances
the most.

Yes

Yes, I'm a Muslim
but here are some other facts about me:

My favourite food is peanut butter
with banana and coconut

I love my children
in their pyjamas
and pattering bare feet

I know
what it's like to love
till it hurts
I know pain
and loss
I was there when my father
took his last breath

I don't know
how to tell funny anecdotes
I always end up doubled-over
unable to speak
laughing at my own story
while everyone shakes
their heads
and laughs
not at my story
but at my laughter
instead.

Ambassador (Not)

I do not
represent
1.8 billion
a quarter of the earth
I make mistakes
I say and write things
a few million
give or take
may disagree with
but I can say this:
most of the Muslims I know are
hardworking
child-rearing
simple
peaceful
people
who live and die
without ever making it to the news.

A friend:
These poems are nice, but one might ask
Do you represent the typical Muslim?

Me:
What's a typical Muslim?
What's a typical Christian? Atheist?
Arab? American?

What's a typical anything?
And do *you* represent *them?*

If You Could Read Us

You write backwards!
someone said
I laughed:
different
does not mean backwards

I do not write backwards
I just write from the right
which for me
is right
it all depends on perspective
where you see
the beginning
and the end

And if only you could read
my Arabic writing
if only you could read us
you'd read of love
we have a dozen and more
words for love
so nuanced must be
our description of
what lies in our hearts

If you could read us
you'd fall in love
with the curves
of our cursive letters
You'd read:

beauty
and sorrow
and art
and peace.

The Veil

So...
let me get this straight:
I can cover my head...
if I'm a surgeon
cancer patient
or a bride

In sports like diving
or fencing
hair can hide
but I can't veil it
cuz I'm modest
simply shy?!

You say:
It's for your freedom
but you lie!
come on admit it
but look me in the eye

It's about the
"Them" versus "Us"
the great divide

When you strip off my clothes
you are liberating me?!
No! My liberty
is in letting me decide!

Go ahead
do your worst
you'll know real beauty
in my defiance
in my strength and pride.

Under the Influence

I am no more
oppressed by my veil
than other women (or I)
might be by:
high heels
flowing skirts
long nails
butterfly lashes
and endless cosmetics

Or by:
cargo pants
or clunky boots
for that matter

All arguably
heavy
inconvenient

All definitely
promoted by culture
not always a culture of religion, perhaps
but a culture nonetheless
of fashion
beauty
feminism
expectations of what a woman should be

I may be under some influence
but then we all are
and as long as we are aware
It's still a choice.
So, please. Just back off.

Full exposure
and full coverage
can both objectify
not that
anyone
has the right
to objectify
Us

The point is not
what we wear
or not
but that we
put it on
or take it off
as a matter
of respect
choice
and freedom.

Sanctuary

Do you know what a sanctuary is?
It's a door that squeaks
and stairs that creak
under the weight of your feet

Bare walls
a curtain torn
mismatched carpets
threadbare and worn

An open window
that lets in the breeze
and birdsong
but keeps out the world's cruelty

A mattress in the corner
and running water
a place named after a woman
Aisha,[8] meaning "a woman alive"
a place for women only
to shed their layers
... and their tears

This is my mosque
where I wandered one day
because I needed walls to cover my raw, open wounds
where I doubled-over on the ground

---

[8] Mosques are often named after people. Aisha was Prophet Mohammad's wife.

the mattress was too high
wondering if I'd ever breathe normally again

Where I fell asleep
something I'd not done in days
and woke up to the sound of my own laughter
and the fading image of a silly face in my dreams
(I have a weakness for silly faces)

This is my sanctuary
and heartbreakingly
it was labelled on a map
as a terrorist centre[9]

Really?
well, it is *not*
a terrorist centre
it is *my* centre
cuz when my world tipped over its axis
this "centre"
"centred" me.

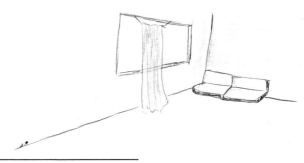

---

[9] This label was reported and removed from the map.

God

When I am close to God
no one else matters
nothing else matters

I am invincible
by association

My soul came from His
I knew Him before I came to this earth
even though I don't remember knowing Him

I will meet Him again
after I leave

And in between
in this short spark of a life
I seek to know Him
to remember Him
in this distracting world

When I have these glimpses of clarity
enlightenment
I think:
what harm can befall me?
and what does it matter?

My soul is immortal
and it's only a matter of years
or days
before I get to go

Home
to real life
to Him.

Fifty-three people prayed in a mosque[10]
on a quiet peaceful night
twenty-five were shot
nineteen injured
six killed

Shot
as they prayed
heads bowed
defenceless

My husband's friend
had just moments ago left.
My husband said:
Wid, it could have been *any one of us*
Then, in an attempt
to bring people together
someone organized a
come-meet-a-Muslim event
ask them anything you want
see how human they are
how harmless
don't touch
It was a good event
they meant well
I spoke well
but

---

[10] "Quebec City Mosque Shooting." Wikipedia. Accessed April 2, 2019. https://en.wikipedia.org/wiki/Quebec_City_mosque_shooting.

All the time I wondered
how was it that
I was the one shot at
yet *I* am the one on trial
or display
answering questions
alleviating fears
telling *you*
not to be afraid
of *me*

Note

I almost removed this poem
don't want to bother anyone
or make anybody uncomfortable
God forbid
Then
Christchurch[11] happened
another 50 killed
Mucad was 3 years old
The poem stays

[11] See "Christchurch Mosque Shootings: The Faces of the Victims." NZ Herald. Accessed March 16, 2019. https://www.nzherald.co.nz/nz/news/article.cfm?c_id=1&objectid=12213358.

White Veil

You think I'd never take
my white veil off
but you're wrong
I swear I would take it off
to stop your bleeding
or to tie you down
if you were going to hurt yourself
I'd throw it over the ledge
to pull you back up
if you fell

to keep you alive

I might take it off
if I thought you'd otherwise
turn it into a noose around my neck

to survive

But since
none of these events
are happening today
thankfully
I will keep it on
and wave its dangling edge
a peace flag
an olive branch

to say Hi.

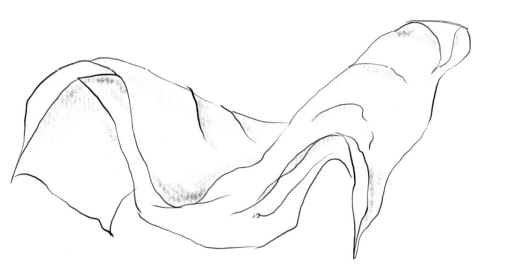

Forgive me
for being so defensive
I've been accused for so long
and so many times
I forget
that you never attacked me.

Terroriste

I was walking by the canal
one beautiful cloudy day
pushing my baby girl
in her hand-me-down orange stroller
I was content
and happy
and humming

Then suddenly
from across the water
he flung the word at me: *'TERRORISTE!'*
which somehow sounded worse in the feminine form
he mumbled words before and after
but I could no longer hear
for the ringing in my ears

I said to my baby
(but more to myself):
It's okay, it's okay, it's okay

And he went on his way
so casually finishing his bike ride
in his cool athletic gear

He was not terrorized at all
I was.

On My Mat

Child's pose
forward fold
hand on heart
eyes are closed
finding peace
breathing slow

Beautiful
if called yoga
good for you
if called meditation

But what if
I called it
my daily Muslim prayer
my five-times-a-day
connection to God?

Could you
still see it
as the beautiful
peaceful
unthreatening
not ignorant
not backward
not naive
progressive
flow
that
it
is?

It never ceases to amaze me
how determined the world is
to vilify
or at least
ignore you

You, who are ranked number 1
in Michael Hart's
The 100
A ranking of the most
influential people in history[12]

Yet
every spiritual
or leadership
or self-help book
goes from Socrates
to Jesus
to Buddha
to modern psychology
and neuroscience
they skim over you completely

[12] Michael Hart. *The 100: A Ranking of the Most Influential Persons in History.* New York: Citadel Press, 1992.

You
who have left behind
in your teachings
and in the way you lived
such pearls of wisdom

One pearl:
wherever you find wisdom
whomever it comes from
whatever its source
take it
just take it[13]

Peace be upon you:

Mohammad

---

[13] "The wise statement is the lost property of the believer, so wherever he finds it, then he is more worthy of it." (Sunnah.com. Accessed April 2, 2019. https://sunnah.com/urn/628980.)

The Muslim Golden Age

The Dark Ages
were not dark
all over the world

When the sun sets somewhere
it shines in other places

It just depends where you're standing.[14]

---

[14] For more knowledge about the Muslim Golden age, see "1001 Inventions: Discover a Golden Age – Inspire a Better Future." Accessed April 2, 2019. http://www.1001inventions.com/.

I'm so busy
defending myself
I forget to say
what I'd say
if you simply asked:
what is Islam, anyway?

I am so wrapped up
in telling you
what it is not
that I forget
to tell you
everything
it is.

Shahada

I testify
I say out loud to the world
that I believe
there is only one God
and that Mohammad
is His messenger

This simple belief
is what makes me a Muslim

In Arabic, *shahada* means "testimony".

Salah

I pray
five times a day
it helps me stay

connected

In Islam, this prayer is called
Salah:
from *silah*
or "connection".

Zakah

I give alms
money to the poor
it's not charity
but their right
to their portion
of my wealth[15]

Share the goods
have compassion
be human

In Islam
this giving is called
Zakah:
to cleanse and elevate oneself
of greed
and other ailments
of the heart.

---

[15] In Islam, alms are 2.5% of wealth.

Sawm

I fast
don't eat or drink
or gossip
or swear
from dawn until dusk
the night is mine

Repeat for the length of the lunar month of
Ramadan

In Islam, this fasting is called
Sawm: abstinence
abstain from your desires
don't always be a slave to them
cultivate your discipline.

Hajj

Once in your lifetime
if you are able
go to Mecca for Hajj:
the pilgrimage

Come to Mecca and
endure the heat
the crowds
be barefoot
be humble
be plain
dress in simple white

Lose your status
forget your race
and join
the one human race
be inconvenienced
see how others live

Meet your brothers and sisters
from around the world
know each other
see each other

And once your worshiping is done
but before you leave
there is no harm in
doing some trade and business

After all
Islam is not a religion
of monks and mosques
It's one
of life and living.

If Islam Should Speak:

There are things you don't know
about me
like how
my name
is pronounced

The *s*
in Islam
does not sound
like the *s*
in *is*
It's soft
like in *soft*
and the *l*
is not heavy
like in *lie*
or *low*
but light
like in
lumiere
or *l'amour*

Islam
say it softly
it means in Arabic:
surrender

That's just my name
a starting point
please join me
and wonder
what else we don't know
about each other.

If You Knew Me

You would never have shot me
or beaten me to the ground
if you knew me

If you knew me
you'd never have been angry or afraid
if you knew me
you'd have *loved me*
you'd have shed more tears for me
than this blood on your hands

I think you know it
yet cannot bear to know it
so you avoid my gaze
as the life leaves my body
you may look at me
but you don't *see me*

if you saw me
you'd have seen yourself.

Other

I am not   an "other"
I am just   another
      brother.

Heaven

I am but a traveller
in this life
enjoying the journey
and tolerating it
but so looking forward
to reaching
home.

Closing

And in the end
I hope that I
did not offend
it's hard to always be

poetically correct.

Finishing this book feels like coming home, like winding down after a long journey, like kicking off my shoes and resting my hat/s on that little table many of us have by the door. I'm happy it's done but already nostalgic. I'll leave you with some of my hopes:

I hope you heal
from what ails you
I hope the scars
in your heart will close
I hope your heart itself
will stay open
I hope you grow
into your own greatness
I hope you learn
how to be kind to yourself
I hope you'll see
the human
in every person you meet
I hope you find
what you're looking for
I hope
you've done
some of all
of that
already
right here
with me.

AFTERWORD

Dear Reader,

These words I'm writing now are literally *after*-words. They came to me after the final draft of the book was written. Sometimes we only understand a story at the very end, we only appreciate a view after climbing to the very top, we only discover ourselves after traveling the world, then coming full circle to find our answers right here at home, or even within ourselves.

That is the case for me with this book. My whole view of why and how it came to being shifted as I circled closer and closer to end. But let me start from the beginning. The actual writing of these poems took several years. They started out as little seeds in my notes, then became a blog, then seemed to gain momentum until they took on a life of their own and insisted on becoming a book. I couldn't explain it to myself or others; I just felt compelled to keep writing and knew that the book was simply: coming.

It wasn't easy. There were starts and stops and dry spells where I called my sister to say, 'The book is dying! It will never see the light of day!' And that thought filled me with grief, as if my book were a living thing, like a baby. Then it would come alive again and keep me up at night, writing and illustrating and searching for publishers (thank you, Austin Macauley).

Then, as a semi-final draft was being reviewed by my editor, I attended a workshop titled: Daring Greatly™, which is a highly experiential methodology based on the research of Brené Brown, PhD, LMSW. The workshop addressed courage, vulnerability, and shame resilience. This was a clear case of 'When the pupil is ready, the master appears.' I had finished the book, was quite happy with how it was going, and was ready to dedicate some time to "me" during this course. Then, the discussion on the second day of the workshop drove home an idea I had just begun to grasp from Brené's talks and books:

The idea that our identities are intricately woven into our stories, and that when we deny parts of our stories, we deny parts of *ourselves*. We cut off, we *orphan* parts of ourselves that don't fit with how we want the world to see us. But to feel worthy and whole and authentic, we must own all the facets of our stories, and of our selves.

This "truth" hit me like a ton of bricks. There was this glimmer of recognition, understanding, and a heartbreaking remembering of *my orphans:* all those parts of me that were shut out and locked away. I wanted to say, 'Wait, wait, wait, stop. What?!'

I went home straight to bed and had so little energy the next few days. And I cried. I wasn't depressed. I was in awe and in peace, and I needed time to process and absorb this idea that reframed my past so that I could now read it in such a different, much-softer light. My story was becoming clearer.

The book was my story. The chapters were my orphans, parts of myself hidden away because they did not fit the persona I wanted or needed to present to the world.

I started to greet my orphans: the individual, different, quirky, rebellious child who learned to appease, please, charm and dissipate anger from a distance. The feminine woman who put on her pants to become a man in a man's world. Tough, not too loud, not too pretty. The romantic who did not know if the world could handle the idea of a reserved yet passionate woman. The human who has all the pains and insecurities of other human beings yet wonders what her colleagues and clients would say if they knew: I feel down sometimes, too.

Seeing the facets of myself (or my hats) as orphans has infused me with a desire to protect them, own them, and allow them to be seen—even if my being complex and contradictory confuses people, offends them, or defies their expectations. I began to understand the urgency behind the book; it was never a frivolous project to pass the time. It was an act of healing and of self-integration.

As I end this book, I begin the journey of owning all of my story, of embracing this unfamiliar liberating realisation that I do not need to defend who I am or announce which hat I'm wearing each minute and that I can rest and just... be. I understand now that what started as an ambitious journey to connect with others, ended up being a humble journey to connect with myself.

Hoping to have connected with you anyway ;)

and that you

might have

connected

with yourself

Sincerely,

Wid.